A Devotional for the Journey

By Dr. Kim Grom
Illustrated by Justin Redmond

Reflections of Grace: A Devotional for the Journey
© 2023 by Dr. Kim Grom

All rights reserved. No part of this book may be reproduced without written permission from the publisher or copyright holder, nor may any part of this book be transmitted in any form or by any means electronic, mechanical, photocopying, recording, or other, without prior written permission from the publisher or copyright holder.

Unless otherwise noted, all scriptural quotations are taken from the New King James Version®. Copyright © 1982 by Thomas Nelson. Used by permission. All rights reserved.

Illustrated by Justin Redmond.

ISBNs: 978-1-7344895-4-5 (Paperback)

   978-1-7344895-6-9 (Hardcover)

   978-1-7344895-3-8 (Ebook)

This devotional is dedicated to my mother, Gail.
Her pragmatic nature, kindness, and faith has been appreciated.
For these qualities, along with the sacrifices she has made, including that of being my mother, I am forever grateful.

Reflections of Grace

Through your lonely and darkest times, have you felt God's comforting hand upon you? His love is there in the whisper of His name.

Fear not, for I am with you; be not dismayed, for I am your God. I will strengthen you, yes, I will help you, I will uphold you with My righteous right hand.
Isaiah 41:10

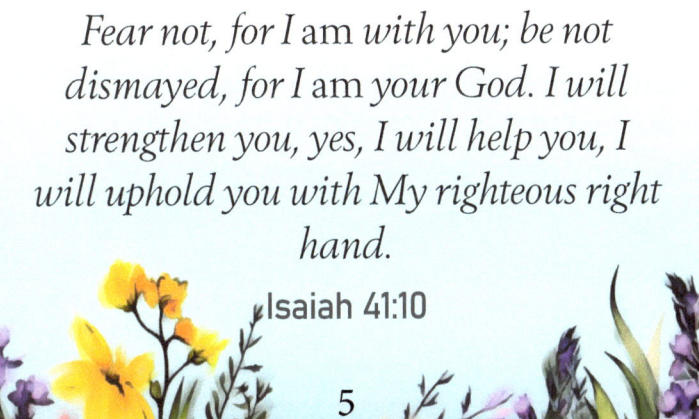

Reflections of Grace

Can you remember the day you knew you knew you were redeemed? No one and nothing else could save you! You will never be the same.

But as many as received him, to them He gave the right to become children of God, to those who believe in His name.
John 1:12

Reflections of Grace

You are not just redeemed, but you are also deeply loved. You are a son and a daughter of the King. Your lineage is that of royalty.

But you are *a chosen generation, a royal priesthood, a holy nation, His own special people, that you may proclaim the praises of Him who called you out of darkness into His marvelous light.*
1 Peter 2:9

Reflections of Grace

As new life unfolds you learn God's ways. He guides you in matters of the heart and provides new direction.

I will instruct you and teach you in the way you should go; I will guide you with My eye.

Psalm 32:8

Reflections of Grace

At times—maybe often—you may feel like you are walking alone. But when you are alone with God, His love and mercy will comfort you in ways you never imagined.

Fear not, for I am with you; be not dismayed, for I am your God. I will strengthen you, yes, I will help you, I will uphold you with My righteous right hand.

Isaiah 41:10

Reflections of Grace

The healing love and grace of God are yours. He is your healer. Your body and soul may be broken, yet He restores you.

The Lord is my shepherd; I shall not want. He makes me to lie down in green pastures; He leads me beside the still waters. He restores my soul.

Psalm 23:1-3

"For I will restore health to you And heal you of your wounds" says the Lord.

Jeremiah 30:17

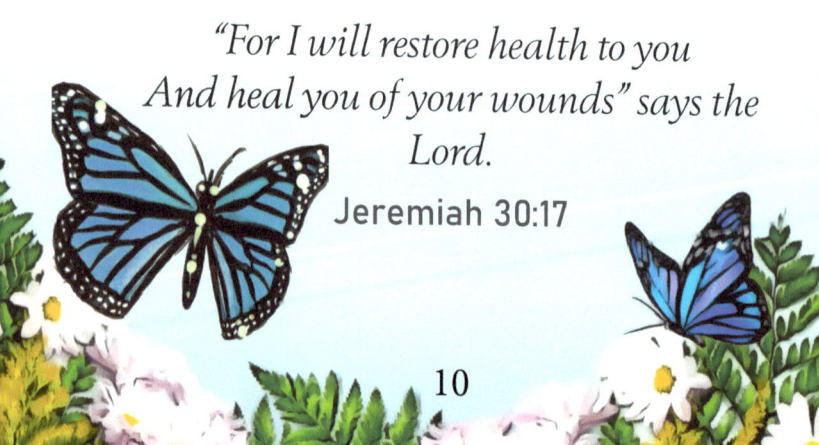

Reflections of Grace

His yoke is easy and His burden is light. Worship, prayer, and reading the Bible are a blessing to partake of. He does the rest.

He has shown you, O man, what is good. And what does the Lord require of you? But to do justly, to love mercy, and to walk humbly with your God.

Micah 6:8

Reflections of Grace

You will endure persecution and offenses, but be of good cheer! Jesus has overcome. He has the victory over sin, death, and the enemy.

Now thanks be to God who always leads us in triumph in Christ.
2 Corinthians 2:14

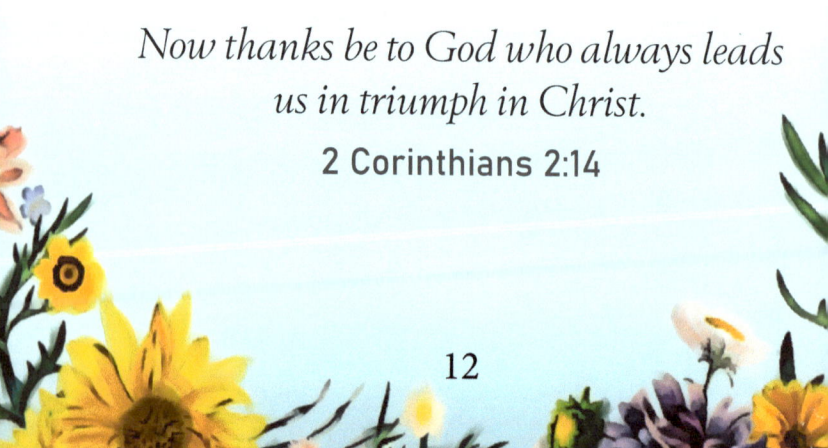

Reflections of Grace

God is sovereign; He rains on the just and the unjust. He will have mercy and favor on whom He chooses—and He chose you. Rejoice!

You did not choose Me, but I chose you and appointed you that you should go and bear fruit, that your fruit should remain, that whatever you ask the Father in My name He may give you.
John 15:16

Reflections of Grace

As you endure trials and tribulations, trust in Him. He sees it all, and He is your deliverer!

The Lord is my rock and my fortress and my deliverer; my God, my strength, in whom I will trust; My shield and the horn of my salvation, my stronghold. I will call upon the Lord, who is worthy to be praised; so shall I be saved from my enemies.

Psalm 18:2-4

Reflections of Grace

Press in to God when you are going through trials. Cherish those times because God is able to rescue you. You are an overcomer!

But may the God of all grace, who called us to His eternal glory by Christ Jesus, after you have suffered a while, perfect, establish, strengthen, and settle you.
1 Peter 5:10

Reflections of Grace

Embrace the changes that come as you progress from glory to glory. Sanctification is not easy, but it is glorious!

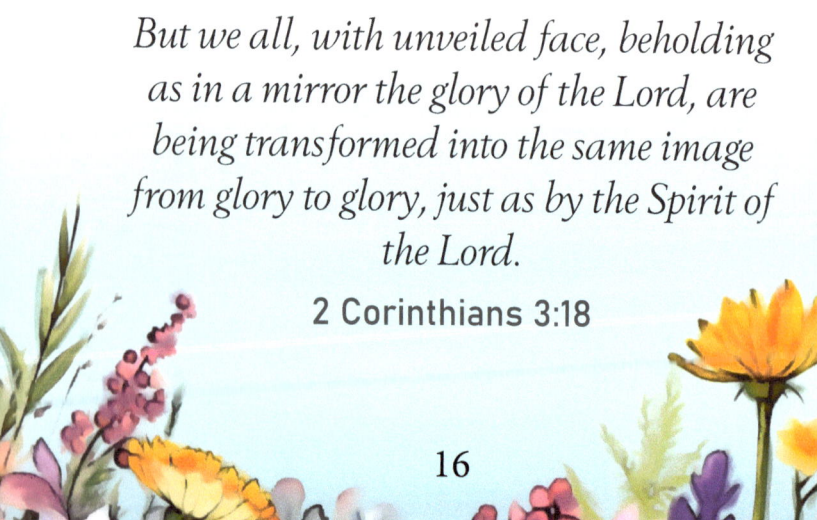

But we all, with unveiled face, beholding as in a mirror the glory of the Lord, are being transformed into the same image from glory to glory, just as by the Spirit of the Lord.
2 Corinthians 3:18

Reflections of Grace

There is no law against walking in the fruit of the Spirit. Wear it like a beautiful garment.

But the fruit of the Spirit is love, joy, peace, longsuffering, kindness, goodness, faithfulness, gentleness, self-control. Against such there is no law.

Galatians 5:22-23

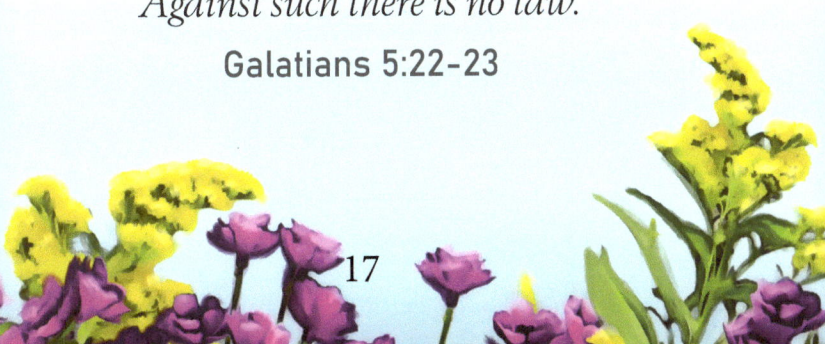

Reflections of Grace

Patiently learn to love others without compromising the truth. The truth is what sets us free.

Teach me Your way, O Lord; I will walk in Your truth; unite my heart to fear Your name.

Psalm 86:11

Reflections of Grace

Accept the chastening of the Lord. Parents discipline their children so they will make better choices and to build their character. Abba Father chastens those He loves.

If you endure chastening, God deals with you as with sons; for what son is there whom a father does not chasten?

Hebrews 12:7

Reflections of Grace

Speaking the truth in love is not an easy task, but it bears fruit. The truth of His Word will not return void.

So shall My word be that goes forth from My mouth; it shall not return to Me void, but it shall accomplish what I please, and it shall prosper in the thing for which I sent it.

Isaiah 55:11

Reflections of Grace

Keep the Lord's day holy. Faith comes as we hear the Word of God. Make sure to stay connected with other believers in church and outside of church to build your faith.

Remember the Sabbath day, to keep it holy.
Exodus 20: 8

Reflections of Grace

Fellow believers are our counterparts in the body of Christ. Life is better lived when we are at harmony with other believers.

For we, though many, are one bread and one body; for we all partake of that one bread.

1 Corinthians 10:17

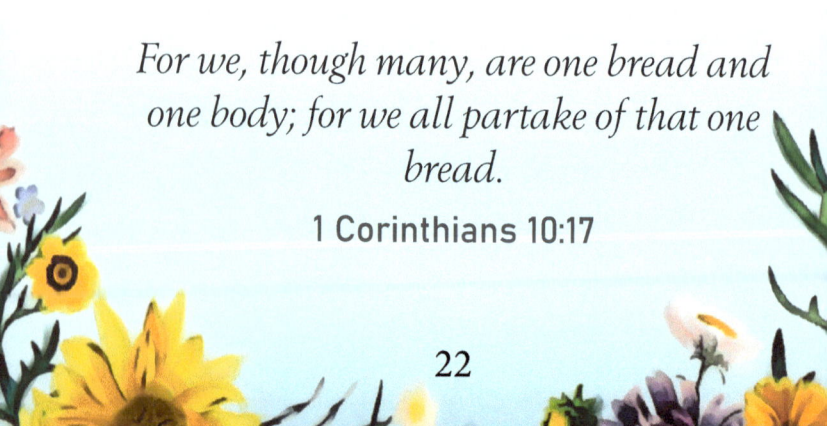

Reflections of Grace

There are no grandchildren in the body of Christ. Each person has to decide for themselves to follow Jesus. Choice determines one's eternal destiny. What a joy it is to be a heaven-bound child of the King!

If you confess with your mouth the Lord Jesus and believe in your heart that God has raised Him from the dead, you will be saved.

Romans 10:9

Reflections of Grace

Walking with Jesus is a rich and rewarding way to pass through this life. Blessings not received in this lifetime will be yours for eternity. Do not despair.

Whoever drinks of the water that I shall give him will never thirst. But the water that I shall give him will become in him a fountain of water springing up into everlasting life.

John 4:14

Reflections of Grace

Ask, seek, and knock. Cast all your cares upon Him, for He cares for you.

Casting all your care upon Him, for He cares for you.
1 Peter 5:7

Reflections of Grace

Love covers a multitude of sins. Through it all, God keeps us securely in the palm of His hand and watches over us.

The Lord shall preserve you from all evil; He shall preserve your soul. The Lord shall preserve your going out and your coming in from this time forth, and even forevermore.

Psalm 121: 7-8

Reflections of Grace

Give Him the sacrifice of praise. Offer Him praise and worship, for He is worthy!

Great is the Lord, and greatly to be praised; and His greatness is unsearchable. One generation shall praise Your works to another, and shall declare Your mighty acts. I will meditate on the glorious splendor of Your majesty, and on Your wondrous works.

Psalm 145:3-5

Reflections of Grace

Life is short. Eternity is forever. God is good. Let these truths encourage you!

For the Lord is good; His mercy is everlasting, and His truth endures to all generations.

Psalm 100:5

About the Author

An avid gardener, Dr. Kim Grom especially loves English style gardening. Scriptural meditations are one of her favorite pastimes. Kim can be reached at www.drkimgrom.org.

Other Books by Dr. Kim Grom

The Promise within the Garden

The Promise within the Garden will draw you deeper and closer to the heart of God. Page after page unfolds a beautiful descriptive journey along with lovely renderings of old European gardens. Accompanied by scriptural meditations and contemplations about the inner workings of nature, readers can use the book as a personal devotional or it is a wonderful book to give to someone who enjoys flowers and gardening. Start reading now to find *The Promise within the Garden*!

www.ingramcontent.com/pod-product-compliance
Lightning Source LLC
Chambersburg PA
CBHW041807160426
43209CB00015B/1716